"I'm amazed at how many time management courses talk about the ability to change time and reality. I say rather, 'Embrace reality and see what you can do to take advantage of it.'"

"The key is action. Pick the ideas and strategies that apply to you. Then take action and make them work!"

Getting Organized
at Work

24 Lessons to Set Goals, Establish
Priorities, and Manage Your Time

KENNETH ZEIGLER

McGRAW-HILL

New York Chicago San Francisco Lisbon
London Madrid Mexico City Milan New Delhi
San Juan Seoul Singapore Sydney Toronto

The *McGraw·Hill* Companies

6 7 8 9 0 DOC/DOC 0 9 8 7 6

ISBN 0-07-145779-8

 This book is printed on recycled, acid-free paper containing a minimum of 50% recycled, de-inked fiber.

McGraw-Hill books are available at special quantity discounts to use as premiums and sales promotions, or for use in corporate training programs. For more information, please write to the Director of Special Sales, Professional Publishing, McGraw-Hill, Two Penn Plaza, New York, NY 10121-2298 or contact your local bookstore.

To order
Getting Organized at Work
call 1-800-842-3075

Contents

☑ *Organize for success!*

*T*he goal of this book is to provide tips, tools, ideas, and strategies that you can apply and see immediate, measurable improvement, both at work and at home. This book will help you use whatever system you're currently using more effectively.

Many time management courses talk about the ability to change time and reality. That seems impractical. Instead of acting like the salmon and swimming against the current, go with the flow—but add structure and discipline.

This book is intended to get you to analyze your use of time and answer this question: *Why* are you doing *what* you're doing *when* you're doing it?

Follow these three steps:

1. Keep track of your time (work and personal) for a week. It may surprise you to find out how much time tasks and activities take.
2. Then, analyze your findings. Identify any activities that are unnecessary and eliminate them.
3. Find or create times that you could block off for important tasks or activities that have a high payoff. Sometimes these tasks and activities get delayed because of things that are relatively less important or even unnecessary.

Once you keep track of your time for a week, you should see patterns in activities, tasks, interruptions, and unplanned events. Once you see those patterns, use the strategies discussed in this book to handle them more effectively.

The key is action. Pick two or three ideas or strategies at a time and work on them until they become a habit. Then pick two or three more and work on them until they become a habit. At the end of every week, ask yourself what you could do better next week. In addition, realize that there are two aspects to saving time:

- Improving your time management skills
- Training others so their time management skills don't interfere with yours.

"This book is for anyone who would like to become more efficient, get more done in less time, and have balance in their life."

☑ *Take control of your day*

Your life is like a circus. You can be the ringmaster or you can be the beast. You can manage your day or let your day manage you. It's basically a matter of discipline. To take control of your day, you have to:

- Change your thought process. You have more control than you think, but you must take action and negotiate your way through the day.
- Be more patient. You need to slow down, instead of running around like a chicken with its head cut off.
- Acquire more discipline. Realize that "There's a time and a place for everything." Without discipline, you'll jump from task to task and wonder at the end of the day, "Where did today go?"

Here are some examples of how you can take control of your day.

Train others to be more efficient in making their requests: Even if you have excellent time management skills, your coworkers will still make your life difficult because of their poor time management skills. Whether they call, drop by your office, or send e-mails, they should provide enough specific information to allow you to help most efficiently.

Also realize that you are part of the problem. Be more specific in how you communicate with others. Lead by example.

Train others to manage their time, too: Apply the strategies suggested in this book. Remember: when you manage your time better, you're also showing those around you how to manage their time better. It's in your best interests to train the people around you to recognize that there's a time and a place for everything—and it's not necessarily "right here and right now."

It's nice to keep your door open, but it's smart to control interruptions. Work at deferring the matters with which others interrupt you and scheduling a time and a place for them.

Complete more tasks instead of jumping around: When you get a request, try to fit it in where it works best for you and still works for the requestor. Multitasking may be a necessity, but it's not generally a virtue. In fact, it's often an inefficient way to allow *time* to manage *you*.

Do one thing at a time, like successful people do: Be a traffic cop. Just as a typical traffic cop stands in an intersection and indicates which vehicles should go and which vehicles should stop, direct the flow of work that comes through your office and across your desk.

"To become a ringmaster, you must realize that there's a time and a place for everything. Successful time managers realize that it's all about discipline."

☑ *Set goals*

*T*he first step in managing your time is to know what you need or want to accomplish.

A goal is the end result toward which you direct time, energy, and resources. It should define the outcome and the purpose.

Why set goals?

- Goals give meaning to time management.
- Goals provide clear focal points for action.
- Goals identify specific opportunities for improved results.
- Goals establish a clear picture or direction for achieving those results.
- Goals improve performance by setting accountability for results.
- Goals provide structure for achieving the results you want.
- Goals improve communication by promoting mutual agreement on expectations.
- Goals provide a fair way to reward success.

The first step in setting goals is to see them in your mind. Close your eyes and picture what the task or project will look like when you reach it—the result. Then, work backwards and write as you go. A major problem is that people tend to leave out steps. You reduce the chances of doing this if you can really see the result in your mind.

Notice that I advise, "Write as you go." There's a direct correlation between the amount that you write about your task or project and the probability of succeeding at it: the more you write, the greater your commitment and the higher the probability of success.

Why? Because writing helps you clarify: your tasks or projects and your goals become more real as you put them into black and white. And, because we're visual, seeing your words makes your commitment more obvious.

Then, as you complete each task or part of a project, check it or cross it off. Visual proof of completing tasks makes you feel successful. The more you write down, the more you will complete and the more successes you will achieve. When you don't write down all of the steps as you plan, you won't be getting all of the credit you deserve.

These three points are essential to setting goals:

Understand how your job fits into the bigger picture: Know the goals of your team, your business unit, and your organization. Then, decide how you should be helping achieve those goals.

Know what's important to your leader: Your boss signs your paycheck, evaluates your performance, and decides on raises and promotions. So, what matters most to the person who matters most? If you don't know what's important to your boss, how are you prioritizing?

Ask your internal and external customers about their expectations: You're likely to get valuable insights about what results you should target with your goals.

"You've got to be careful if you don't know where you're going, because you might not get there."
—Yogi Berra

☑ *Think realistically*

***W**hat's* the number-one reason why people don't achieve their goals or meet their deadlines on time? Reality! They haven't left any room for anything to go wrong, for interruptions, for the unexpected.

That's why it's so important to try to anticipate potential obstacles or changes from the start or at least before they occur. That's why it's important to review your progress constantly and check with team members. Identify any problems as early as possible and devise a plan to avoid or resolve each problem.

It's good to be optimistic, but sometimes when setting goals people act as if nothing has ever gone wrong. It's essential to be realistic and acknowledge the possibility of problems. In fact, you should look for all problematic possibilities—and then develop contingency plans.

When someone gives you a project, ask as many questions as necessary at the start, to understand the project and what's expected as well as possible. Some projects may require that you make assumptions. If so, share those assumptions with whoever gave you the project. Then, at the end of each week, review your assumptions and be prepared to make changes.

When you allow room in your plan for things to go wrong, you can be more confident that you'll meet your deadlines and achieve your goals. Then, you can be optimistic—realistically.

In order to complete a project on time, it's important to believe that you can do it. Make sure your goals are achievable and your time frame is realistic. It's better to under-promise and over-deliver than to over-promise and under-deliver.

What if you can't do a project? First, don't complain to whoever gave you the project. No one likes a complainer. Come up with a solution, an alternative plan. Then, talk with that person. Explain why you don't consider the project realistic and then offer your solution.

When you take on a project, do the following:

Take advantage of your experience: Think about any past projects that have been similar in any way. How can you use those experiences to plan the new project and to make it succeed?

Analyze problems from the past: What went wrong with those projects? Keep in mind the wise words of George Santayana—"Those who cannot remember the past are condemned to repeat it." Avoid repeating problems that plagued projects in the past.

Consider what resources you will need: What things and what people are necessary? What and who might be useful?

"Communicate your expectations to others so they know what they will need to do to help you achieve your goals. Also, ask them what they will need of you and your group to achieve their goals."

☐ Start now

☑ *Plan your work*

Some people tend to just jump into tasks and projects immediately. Others tend to put them off. (Conventional wisdom supports both approaches: "He who hesitates is lost" and "Haste makes waste.")

Procrastination is obviously a problem, of course—which we'll discuss in the next lesson. But it's also a problem to spring into action without planning appropriately, for two reasons. We all know about the dangers of taking the "ready, fire, aim" approach: we make mistakes and create problems, sometimes wasting resources and frustrating others. But there can be problems when people leap enthusiastically into a project—and then slow down or stop completely as they get overwhelmed by it.

Both problems—procrastinating and plunging—can be avoided or overcome in the same way: through planning.

The number-one reason why people put off tasks and projects is that the work seems too involved and too difficult. That's why the most effective approach is the ancient military strategy of divide and conquer.

Break large tasks and projects into chunks that you can manage—the more difficult the work, the smaller the chunks. We've all heard the wisdom that "the longest journey begins with a single step." Make it a small step, as easy and/or as quick as possible. If you feel overworked and stressed, maybe you feel unable to commit to more than 15 minutes. If so, then plan a first step that should take you about that long. If your schedule is so tight for the near future that you feel tempted to put off a project, break it into chunks that will each take an amount of time that you can commit to each day.

For each piece of the project, identify the outcome(s) desired, the reason(s), and the time frame, with a deadline. The more specific you make your plan, the more realistic each task becomes and the more logically you can organize those tasks.

These three suggestions should also help you plan your work effectively:

Write your plan out in detail: The more you break down a project, the more writing you'll do—and the easier the project will seem at the start and the easier it will actually be as you take each of the steps.

Communicate: This is a key factor in planning tasks and projects and then achieving your goals. As advised earlier, communicate your expectations to others so they know what they will need to do to help you achieve your goals. Also, communication shows and reinforces commitment.

Create rewards for each step of the project: Success should be rewarded. So, you should set a reward for succeeding in each step of a project, proportionate to the importance of the step.

"A plan without action is a daydream; action without a plan is a nightmare."
—Japanese proverb

☑ *Don't procrastinate*

*T*he number-one way to overcome procrastination is to break down a project and work on it a little every day. But sometimes even the best planning isn't enough to overcome a basic human tendency. We all procrastinate to some degree and in some ways. That's why we must do the following:

- Realize when we're procrastinating and understand why.
- Identify the activities that we prefer to the tasks that we're avoiding.
- Determine steps to manage and overcome our procrastination.

Why do you procrastinate? Do any of the following thoughts seem familiar?

> *The task is unpleasant. The task is difficult. I'm overwhelmed: too many tasks. I'm interrupted too often. I'm not organized enough. I don't have the necessary information. I don't have clear or written goals. I'm not in the mood. I'm not interested in the task. I don't have time now. I don't have the energy now. This isn't due for a while.*

What activities take you from the tasks that you put off? You may have some favorites—and your reasons may be keeping you from making the most of your potential. Take a moment to list the activities that you prefer to do when you have tasks scheduled. You may learn some interesting things about yourself.

Maybe you're motivated by urgency. Many people react to pressure, for various reasons. When the phone rings or there's a knock at the door, they drop what they're doing to deal with the newest request or demand. If there's a fire to put out, they run on adrenaline. Emergencies make them feel vital, even heroic. But people are seldom recognized and promoted for putting out fires: they stay where they are—because there will always be fires. People who can solve the problems that cause the fires are more likely to get promoted, so they can solve hot problems elsewhere.

Depending on the reasons why you procrastinate and the activities that distract you from your scheduled tasks, you should determine specific ways to improve.

Here are three tips to escape the tendency to procrastinate:

Work on the tasks in the morning: You probably have more energy and can focus better at that time. It's tempting to handle all of the urgent matters and then, after you've put out the fires, to turn to the tasks you've scheduled. That's probably the worst time to do them— if you get to them at all.

Motivate yourself from within: Counter the pressures that you feel around you with internal pressure—the importance of your project, the urgency to accomplish each task as scheduled, the appeal of the rewards you set. This strategy is especially effective if you feel that you do your best work under pressure.

Relax: No, don't stop working hard. Just try to be less of an "adrenaline junky." People who intentionally work under pressure thrive on adversity. Those solo heroics may not play very well with those around you and above you.

"Procrastination makes easy things hard, hard things harder."
—*Mason Cooley*

☑ *Use a master list*

*A*fter you've set goals, it becomes easier to prioritize your tasks by order of importance. To make sure that you have time to focus on what's more important, however, you must also make time to take care of the lower-priority items on your list.

Maybe you're using a day planner. Maybe you're using an electronic calendar. It doesn't matter. Our focus here is to improve your organizational skills so that you can use whatever system you're using more effectively and efficiently. That's just being realistic. If organizing doesn't work very well, you'll stop doing it. If organizing takes too long, you'll stop doing it.

The new tools recommended here are not a traditional to-do list. Forget everything you know about a to-do list. Instead learn the two key building blocks of staying organized—the Master List and the Daily List.

In brief, a Master List is a pad of paper where you will keep all the possible activities, notes, action items, etc., for an entire week. A Daily List is one piece of paper where you will plan a realistic number of key activities for that day only. Together, the Master List and the Daily List replace the traditional to-do list.

Here's how to keep a Master List:

1. ***Only have one list:*** A Master List replaces everything else you are using, i.e. Post-it® notes, etc. Your work and personal life all go together in one place, on your Master List.

2. *As thoughts pop into your head, write them down and then forget about them:* This ensures that you don't lose any ideas and you keep your mind free and better able to focus. If you don't have your Master List handy, leave a message on your voice-mail.

3. *Keep the list usable:* Skip lines between entries so you can make notes and it doesn't get cluttered. You should be able to find and read items easily, when you need them or when you're transferring items to your calendar.

4. *Keep a Master List for the whole week:* Rewrite your Master List every Friday. Then, file the old Master List to reference at your annual review.

5. *Create the next day's daily list each afternoon:* Transfer onto it a realistic number of activities from your Master List for that day only.

Here are some final thoughts on using a Master List:

Jot down details: When we're overworked, keeping details is one of the first skills to go, but it's one of the most valuable. Details will save time and prevent misunderstandings. Whether you accept that "the devil is in the details" or "God is in the details" or both, details are crucial.

Make it fast, spontaneous, and loose: Don't try to prioritize or organize the notes at first; this comes later. Think of it as a "brain dump."

Take time at the end of the day to prepare for tomorrow: Fifteen minutes before you leave work each day, don't answer the phone or e-mail and empty as many of your thoughts out of your head as possible, for closure and for a mental separation between work and home. Taking your work home in your head doesn't help your job performance as much as it hurts your personal life. Also, organizing doesn't take much energy, so it's perfect as a final task—a time and a place for everything.

"It is more important to know where you are going than to get there quickly. Do not mistake activity for achievement."
—Mabel Newcomber

☑ *Manage your master list*

*A*s mentioned earlier, don't try to plan as you take notes or at the end of the day. Any planning you do later in the day should be flexible, to allow for changes. Rather, prioritize and organize first thing in the morning, when you arrive and check your memos, voice mail, and e-mail.

Review your Master List throughout the day. Then, at the end of the day, look for items that need to be scheduled. Put them on your Daily List and cross_____ e Master List.

Only _____ t once a week, each Friday. (It's the lowest pro_____ eek.) This way, you focus on a week at a time, _____ rrow. You also save time, since you aren't movi_____" list to a "tomorrow" list at the end of every day_____ is emotionally difficult: you feel discouraged_____ complished enough and you feel greater press_____

Accept th_____ t be crossing off every item on your list by the_____ Reduce the pressure. Don't work late: there's no correlation in productivity between the length of the day and the amount of work accomplished.

On Friday, when you rewrite your Master List, you can evaluate your performance. Then, transfer the items not yet completed to a new Master List. Compare items that you completed and items you're transferring: can you learn anything about your tendencies? Finally, staple the old Master List and file it for future use and review time.

Keep your list handy at all times. This will help reduce "drive-by shootings"—those situations when you're walking somewhere and somebody asks, "Do you have a minute?" With your Master List in hand, you're less likely to try to handle the request immediately. Look at your list and schedule the request appropriately. That's how you develop discipline in your time management. Don't allow requests that pop up to take priority over items on your schedule. Don't reward interruptions and give them control over you.

Here are three suggestions for managing tasks with your Master List:

Use noon as a deadline: That will motivate you to accomplish more in the morning and allow you to feel less pressure later in the day. 90% of all productivity gains occur in the morning.

Apply the "veggie principle": A "veggie" is a task that's good for you and your career or personal life that you put off, probably for late in the day—like vegetables that children avoid eating. Try instead to start each day with a "veggie" and maybe do another before noon.

Balance your Master List with personal items: You need to manage your personal life as well as your work life and it's easier with a single system—and better for you as a whole person.

"People ask me how I got good at managing my time. One week at a time. Each Friday afternoon I look over what I've accomplished for the week and what I could do better the next week and where I could save time."

☑ *Use a daily list*

---

*Y*ou can use your Master List, a day planner, or an electronic planner such as Microsoft Outlook, Lotus Notes, or Novell GroupWise to make a Daily List.

At the end of the day, select two to six tasks from your Master List and put them into your paper Daily List or electronic plan for the next day. The number depends on what meetings, deadlines, and other commitments you have on your schedule already and how much control you have over your day.

The next morning, you may find another two or three tasks in your e-mail and two or three in your voice mail. All together, your day is full.

In your e-mail and voice mail, you're looking only for "veggies"— tasks that are good for you. Compare those with items already on your Daily List.

Then, place a star next to the two biggest "veggies" on your list. Typically, the top two will give you 80% of the value of all of the tasks listed. Build your day around these two tasks and try to "sprinkle" the "fires" around them so you accomplish them.

Try to start the morning with one of them and complete the other before lunch. If you put them off until the afternoon, they'll take some of your time in the morning anyway, because you'll be thinking about them all morning.

Use the other tasks on your Daily List as "filler" around the two main tasks. This will keep you flexible. Try not to move the items on your Daily List to the next day. If that happens, you may be over-planning, being too optimistic for the realities of your situation.

"Fires" pop up and interfere with schedules: it's inevitable. But if you start with a "veggie" and do another by lunch, your day will get much easier, you'll be under less pressure, and those fires won't destroy your schedule. Would you rather have an easy morning and a difficult afternoon, or a difficult morning and an easier afternoon? The choice is really yours.

Manage your day better by following these three suggestions:

Take breaks between tasks: If you take a few moments to refresh yourself and shift gears after each task, you can work more productively.

Work with your concentration cycles: Studies show that our concentration cycles usually last about 90 minutes. At that point, it's wise to take a 10-minute break to recharge. It's a good time to get a drink and/or do an easy or personal task or something you want to do from your Master List.

Maximize your morning: Apply the "veggie" principle and do one or both of your main tasks before lunch. You'll be more focused, have more energy, and (as a result) take less time and make fewer mistakes. Then, your day will flow more smoothly because you got those big tasks out of the way.

"There is no correlation between how long you sit at your desk and what you accomplish."

☑ *Plan for power*

*A*t the end of the day, when you schedule your next day, plan a powerful morning. The average person starts the day by spending one to three hours taking care of e-mail, voice mail, and phone calls and checking in with the boss and others—"relationship building." Reduce this to 15 to 30 minutes so you can get to your first "veggie" sooner. That's discipline!

Check your e-mail and voice mail for "veggies" only. Add them to your list. Then, close your e-mail and turn off the notification, put your phone on voice mail, and jump into your list.

Devote an hour to your biggest "veggie." Defer any interruptions so you can focus. Then, close your "veggie time" and check your e-mail and voice mail and allow interruptions. Take care of the major matters as quickly as possible. Allow 60 minutes to complete as many requests as possible.

Then, shut out e-mail, phone, and interruptions again and take care of your next-biggest "veggie" for 60 minutes. After you finish it, attend to lower-priority e-mails and phone calls. Get back under control before you go to lunch.

Eat lunch after the people who interrupt you the most; that reduces by an hour or two the time in which they can interrupt you. Also, don't work and eat at the same time; in fact, don't eat lunch at your desk.

Use the same approach, structure, and discipline for your afternoon.

By scheduling around your "veggies," batching little tasks (such as phone calls and e-mails), and not letting interruptions and fires control you, you'll be working smarter, not harder. And don't work late: it just makes it harder to return to work on time and fresh for a powerful morning. Spend the last 10-15 minutes planning for the following day.

Monday morning is critical. A good start makes it more likely that the week will be easier and flow better. Don't schedule meetings or conference calls first thing Monday morning.

Don't plan too much. We tend to overestimate by 20%, on average, the amount of time a task will take. Leave room in your schedule for interruptions, last-minute meetings, and unforeseen problems, so you don't run yourself ragged and fail to get everything done.

Use your energy cycles to your advantage: We have at least three energy cycles in a day. For 75% of us, the strongest is the morning, the next strongest is in the afternoon, and the weakest is in the evening. Use your morning more effectively and reduce the chances you'll have to stay late.

Schedule smart: When you plan your day, look for ways to structure it better and work with more discipline. Put the "veggies" in the morning and leave room for interruptions and the unplanned.

Start earlier and leave on time: That's smarter than starting on time and leaving late. You can accomplish more before others arrive—and you can spend more time with your family in the evening. Families notice those who come home late more than those who leave early.

"It took me a long time to realize that others were taking advantage of my best time to get things done. They were reducing my most productive time of the day to a 'pimple'—and I was letting them."

☑ *Prioritize*

*T*he first step in establishing priorities is to keep track of your time for a week, at work and at home. What tasks are you doing and how are you choosing them? Then, you can use the A, B, C method or a decision-making matrix to prioritize tasks.

The A, B, C method is simple.

- An **A** task is one that you *must* do now: *the deadline is today* and the task is *important to your leader,* offers *visibility for you* and your skills, and is *vital to the needs of your customers, peers, or team members.*
- A **B** task is one that you *should* do now: it fits the A criteria but there's no deadline today.
- A **C** task is one that you *like* to do, something that you can work on whenever you have some time to spare.

When you prioritize, you must know why a task is important and when it must be done. Don't assume what people mean by the tone of their voice or who they are in the company. Ask, "When do you really need it?" Conversely, when you're requesting something from others, you must tell them when you need it and why. That helps them prioritize—and better understand what they're committing to do.

The decision-making matrix is similar to the A, B, C method. The upper left square is for time-sensitive, important tasks (A). The upper right square is for important tasks that are not due today (B). The lower left square is for time-sensitive, less important tasks (D). The lower right square is for less important tasks to complete whenever you can (C). The tasks on the left must be completed today; when you plan effectively, you'll be working on tasks in the upper right so they don't end up in the upper left.

That seems easy—on paper. But sometimes, although we have the best intentions, we choose a task for reasons that defy logical criteria. We choose something easy or something that interests us or something that someone is pressuring us to do.

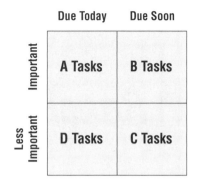

Analyze the tasks that you do first, in order to better understand your motivation. The faster you select and complete the tasks that relate to your goals, your boss, and your key projects, the sooner you can go home.

Also, you're more likely to get raises or promotions for completing your "veggies" than for doing easy tasks or even for putting out fires.

When prioritizing:

Think about each task before you choose to do it: How would you prioritize it with either of the methods explained here? It takes just a few moments to choose smart—and you'll act with greater assurance.

Break down projects into pieces: This advice offered earlier bears repeating here. Because we often tend to do tasks that are easier or that don't take much time, we may procrastinate on projects—unless we break them down into smaller tasks that can compete with the less important tasks.

Know what's important to your leader: That should help you prioritize, if you cannot decide by evaluating tasks in terms of goals.

"The number-one reason why people don't prioritize correctly is that they're trying to prioritize without the necessary information—why it's important and when it must be done."

☑ *Specify and negotiate*

A*s* we stated in the introduction, the key to time management is in this question: *Why* are you doing *what* you're doing *when* you're doing it?

To prioritize properly, you must know why a task is important and when it must be done. Anybody who gives you a task should also give you reasons and a deadline.

If they don't, ask! When you ask for specifics, you're helping people get what they need on time.

Sometimes it seems like every task coming in has the same priority: they're all vital and urgent. In fact, urgency may be the most important reason for doing something.

When someone gives you a task and tells you only that it's "important" and the deadline is "ASAP," you're giving that person control over your time. Or, more likely, if you're getting more than one task at a time, you're giving up all control and leaving your time management up to the personality and/or power of those people and maybe even to playing "eenie, meenie, minie, mo" to choose among the tasks.

If the person insists that his or her task is urgent, try to get a specific deadline. Ask, "When is the latest I could do that for you?" If the deadline is too tight for your schedule, try to negotiate for more time. Even if you think you could do a task ASAP, you should allow for realities. If all goes well, you can deliver early and impress the other person; that's better than agreeing to ASAP and delivering late.

Just as you must have reasons and a deadline done in order to prioritize properly, expect others to prioritize the same way. When you request something from them, say when you need it and why, so they understand what they're committing to do and can prioritize it properly.

When you say, "ASAP" instead of giving a deadline and reasons, the person is likely to take care of your request after tasks that come in with specific deadlines and reasons ... and maybe after tasks that are easier or more interesting. How can they prioritize correctly if they don't know the specific deadline and why it's so important?

Ask questions when people give you a task: Why do they want you to do it? When do they want you to do it? If they don't tell you, ask! If you don't know, how can you prioritize?

Be the ringmaster as a traffic cop: Control the flow of tasks and manage your time effectively and efficiently. You can do that only if you have specific reasons and specific deadlines for doing the tasks coming through your office.

Write down the task and circle the deadline: When you commit to doing a task, keep your word. Not only is it the right thing to do, but if you don't keep your commitments, you're likely to lose negotiating power.

"Successful people have learned to negotiate a way to fit an interruption or a request into their daily plan. Can you create a win-win situation?"

☑ *Focus*

Most people try to do several things at once. However, studies show that successful people do only one thing at a time. They realize that it will take them less time than if they jumped around from task to task. They're able to concentrate better, do the job in less time, and make fewer errors.

Multitasking is often admired as a skill and even cited as a job requirement. In fact, it's usually only an inefficient and ineffective way of dealing with problems resulting from inferior time management. We've appropriated the term from the world of computers: computers multitask, but they're machines—and sometimes when multitasking they freeze up or crash. Focus on one thing at a time: it takes discipline, but the results are worth the effort.

How do you avoid multitasking? Successful people do it in two ways, depending on the importance and urgency of the task that's interrupting.

If the interruption is of a higher priority than the task you're working on, accept it. Jot down any important thoughts or ideas on the current task, make a note of where you are with the task, file it away, and put it back on your list *before* you begin the new request.

If the interruption is less important than the current task, put off the interruption long enough to finish what you're working on. Then, evaluate the second task: it may be less important and urgent than other tasks on your schedule. Remember: successful people try hard to finish their thought, task, or whatever they're working on before they take on a new task or request. That prevents the start/stop, start/stop many people experience all day long.

If you're caught in a situation in which you're tempted to multi-task, here are three suggestions to avoid handling the tasks inefficiently and ineffectively:

Get specifics: Why would you be doing this task? When would be the absolute deadline?

Check your Master List: Rather than accepting a request automatically, look at your Master List and determine the priority that the new task would have.

Consult your boss: When your schedule is full and the person giving you the task is "making you an offer you can't refuse," ask your boss to decide on the order in which you should do the tasks. Sometimes, personality, position, and power compete with priorities.

"Multitasking allows screwing up several things at once."
—e-mail tagline

☑ *Find more time for you*

*I*f you want to get all of your work done so you can go home two hours earlier, you have to eliminate two hours' worth of activities. You won't find all two hours in one place; it will be more like five minutes here and 10 minutes there.

Start by examining how you're spending your time. Look at the tasks on your Master List and your Daily List and consider all unscheduled tasks. For each, ask these two questions:

- Was this the best use of my time?
- Was I doing the right task at the right time?

You should categorize the tasks that you handled:

- Which could have been eliminated?
- Which could have taken less of my time?
- Which could I have delegated?
- Which could I have batched with similar tasks?

This analysis should suggest ways to manage your time better in the future. How could you plan, organize, and prioritize better? Are you working on everything but the right task? Try to be painstakingly honest about what you could improve.

The key for most people is to start with the morning. If you're a morning person, that's where you can make the greatest productivity gains. If not, then look at the afternoon. The early afternoon is best; it's generally a mistake to leave important tasks until the late afternoon or to try to do them after hours.

How could you set up each day so you could start faster, work with more discipline, and get more done in the morning? Organize before you leave work rather than when you arrive. Minimize the time you spend "relationship building" the first thing in the morning.

Here are three recommendations for finding time:

Anticipate problems: Schedule realistically, aware of things that might go wrong, rather than optimistically. You're more likely to do tasks right and not waste time as problems surprise you.

Protect your "veggie" time: You should have two "power hours" every day. I recommend the morning, as I outlined in the lesson "Plan for Power" (pages 17- 18). This is when you should do your "veggies."

Batch similar activities when possible: It may be more efficient to handle (read and write) e-mail, answer voice mail, and make other phone calls in chunks of time—15 minutes as a break or an hour between bigger tasks.

> *"We shall never have more time. We have, and we have always had, all the time there is."*
> —*Arnold Bennett*

☑ *Conquer your desk*

When our desks are cluttered, we lose in at least three ways.

We lose 45 minutes every day, on average, hunting for things on our desks, going through papers and notes. When our desks are cluttered, we lose focus as well as time. Also, we may lose points with our bosses: more and more employees are being evaluated on the appearance of their workspace.

Here are some easy steps to gain control of your desk:

- *Take everything off your desk.* In other words, "zero-base" your desk-top. Wipe it clean for a fresh beginning, like you're just moving in. Then, put things back in the order in which you use them most. What can you do without? Set aside outdated items and pictures. Toss out any candy: it attracts visitors.
- *Put a clock where it will keep you aware of time.* Your perception of time and the reality of it are often different. A watch on the wrist and a time display on the computer are not enough.
- *Organize your tools.* Empty your desk. Cut down on pens, pencils, paperclips, and so forth; try to put them all into one drawer. Keep just a month's supply of stationery. Divide your drawers into separate areas for stationery, files, personal things, etc. Toss any extra stuff you don't really need.

Many people use their desktops as to-do lists. In fact, they may even name their piles. They feel comfortable keeping them close at hand. They believe in the adage, "Out of sight, out of mind."

If you're one of these people, you won't remove those piles

unless you can keep track of each task you need to complete with a Master List or a calendar and you can find your files quickly in file drawers.

We'll get to some suggestions for organizing in the next lesson. But here are three basics for beginning your new order:

Keep only the "present" in your desk file: The best way to overcome paper overload is to manage only the present—what you're working on now and for the next four weeks. You'll focus on organizing the present first.

Set aside the past: Remove from your desk file all files that have been completed or closed out. You'll be using them only for reference.

Set aside the future: Remove from your desk file anything that you expect to be needing or reading in the future. This too will be filed for reference.

> *"Order is the best manager of Time; for unless work is properly arranged, Time is lost."*
> *—Samuel Smiles*

☑ *Control your desk*

*N*ow that you've removed the clutter from your desktop and drawers, you're ready to establish a new order.

Organize the present first. Don't worry about the future or the past until you've organized everything else.

We put off filing because the piles on our desks are usually large and overwhelming and because we worry about being able to find what we need if it's filed. So you need to reduce the piles by filing a little at the end of each day, and you need to set up a filing system that works for you.

Set up your working files in your desk drawer(s) or within arm's length. Organize them alphabetically or chronologically, whichever makes more sense for you.

Limit the categories by keeping them broad. Set up 7 to 10; if you have more, it will take longer to find a file. I'd suggest files for "fingertip info" (phone lists, addresses, and information you use frequently), current projects (a file for each project), routine tasks, clients or prospects, and problems or issues to be researched.

Don't put too many papers in a file or it will take longer to find what you want. Split big files into smaller files for greater convenience. Toss what you no longer need.

As you name each file, think about how you would try to find it later. Make your file names interesting, but logical. Keep them short—not more than three words. Write them in large letters with a marking pen to make the files easy to find.

Use colored file folders to distinguish among your categories so you can find files faster.

Finally, put the future and the past into the reference file. This is a file cabinet that should be located in a corner of your office or just outside.

Handle paper only once. When you handle a paper, note on it the category in which you'll file it: trash, future, past, present, or outbound (sign off or delegate). It cannot stay on your desk.

Don't create clutter. Stop using sticky notes for to-do items. Use your Master List.

Three suggestions to maintain control of your desk:

Have only one thing on your desk at any time: Take out a new file only after you've put the old file away. You'll be less distracted and more able to spread out papers as you work.

File a little every day: If you do, the situation won't get out of hand again. Toss what you don't need. Every Friday, go through your files and get rid of any duplicates or ones you no longer need.

Clean your desk every day: Put your files away. You'll feel more in control—both as you leave and when you arrive. And you won't be worrying about leaving sensitive papers exposed—or any files vulnerable to damage if the sprinklers go off while you're away.

"Order is most useful in the management of everything.... Its maxim is—A place for everything, and everything in its place."

—Samuel Smiles

☑ *Limit interruptions*

---

*T*he average interruption takes six to nine minutes and takes four to five minutes to for recovery. After three or four interruptions your focus and concentration will be gone. Interruptions can take time and affect your focus. To use your time most effectively and efficiently, limit the impact of interruptions.

Discourage visitors by moving your desk or at least your monitor so you're not looking toward the door or windows. Passersby are more likely to drop in if they see your face.

Discourage visitors from staying by removing any extra chairs or putting files on them. Visitors will generally tire of standing and leave.

If possible, keep your door closed during your "veggie" times. Announce and post hours when you'll be available. Set specific times for people who report to you—and promise not to touch the phone or e-mail while they're with you. Put a picture of a "veggie" on your door or a schedule with times when you will and won't be available and a note pad so that people can leave their requests in writing instead of disturbing you.

Try to get out of your office at least three times each morning to ask your team members if they have any questions or need anything. You'll be more visible and they'll have less need to come to your office.

If you can't close your door, escape to a vacant office or meeting room. Tell as few people as possible where you are.

Evaluate each interruption:

■ Is it something you must handle immediately?

- Does it relate to one of your goals, priorities, or key projects?
- Is the request important to the needs of a customer, a peer, or a team member?
- Is it something time-sensitive from your team leader or boss?

If you're not the right person to answer a question or solve a problem, don't try to please: delegate the interruption to the appropriate person.

Develop ways to interrupt interruptions tactfully. The best way to do this without words is to stand up when a visitor arrives. Don't sit down and don't lean. Resist the temptation to get drawn into a conversation. Offer to meet later, to discuss the matter without distractions.

Noise can be an interruption, too. If people gather outside your door, close it or ask them to gather elsewhere. If that doesn't work, headphones might help.

Meetings scheduled by computer can interrupt your other work. If people use a computer to know when you're available, protect your "veggie" time by blocking it on the computer schedule—as a meeting, if necessary.

Analyze recent interruptions for any patterns. How often are you interrupted? When? How? In what specific ways can you control interruptions?

Three more general suggestions:

Respect others: Before interrupting someone, always ask, "Do you have a minute?" Ask others to do the same with you.

Set up a group "power hour": At your next team meeting, suggest designating certain times when interruptions and noise are to be minimized.

Don't interrupt yourself: When working on top-priority tasks, turn off your phone and e-mail. Technology: control it or it controls you.

"Always evaluate your interruptions. Ask yourself, 'Is this truly something I must handle right away?'"

☑ *Manage your e-mail*

E-mails can be especially efficient for requesting information, providing requested information, conveying information, exchanges that should be documented, and communicating with more than one person at a time. But remember: e-mail is technically devoid of tone. It's whatever the reader thinks you meant when he or she opens your e-mail message.

The phone is better when a response is needed immediately, when voices and tones are important to the message, when there's something to discuss, and when privacy is needed.

Set convenient times to check your e-mail. Turn off the notification feature so it doesn't distract you and interrupt your work. Tell people that if they have time-sensitive questions or requests that need a reaction within the hour to call you instead.

When you check your e-mail for the first time each morning, only look for "veggies" that are important and must be done that day. Compare messages with the half-dozen "veggies" that you put on your Daily List the evening before to decide whether a task is a "veggie" or not.

Set your screen to autopreview so you can quickly read the subject line and first three or four lines of the message. After checking your e-mail, set the view to normal.

Set up folders to save messages you want to keep, such as "take action immediately," "pending," "fingertip reference," "meetings," "delegate," and "projects." Within each, set up subfolders. Your e-mail folders and subfolders should match your desk filing system.

Act on e-mails when you read them the first time. Go through all the messages once and delete spam and other wastes of time. Then, act on the most important messages. Finally, file the rest, to keep your inbox clean and save time.

Don't use your inbox as a to-do list: it's like piling papers on your desk. Never have more than one screen of e-mail messages in your inbox. Set up a reminder for the messages you file. Move messages to your calendar as appropriate.

If you note patterns to messages you delete or you file, create filters or rules to block, delete, or route incoming messages directly into the appropriate file folder that you specify. Also, get yourself removed from electronic mailing lists unless you really need to be "in the loop."

Here are three more suggestions for managing your e-mail:

Train others: Ask people to put the reason for the e-mail in the subject line. Then the first three lines should tell what they want and the specific deadline.

Avoid multitasking: Don't write e-mails and talk on the phone at the same time. That way both will take less time and you'll make fewer mistakes.

Reply promptly: Return e-mails the same day. At least acknowledge receipt; otherwise, the sender may call or e-mail until you do. Tell the sender if you'll be away; use the "out-of-office" feature to reply to each e-mail.

"E-mail is the most abused form of communication in the workplace today."

☑ *Master outgoing e-mail*

---

*W*hen sending e-mails, batch them. Give yourself 15 to 30 minutes to send as many as you can or need to send. Then, close your e-mail and move on to your next task. For example, I send most of my return e-mails twice a day, once before lunch and once before I leave for home.

Write e-mails so you get better results faster. The average person decides in 5 to 10 seconds whether to take action, file, or delete an e-mail. Recipients want to know three things:

- Why did I get this e-mail?
- What do I have to do?
- When do you need it?

Before you begin writing, determine the purpose of your e-mail and make a bulleted list of what you need or want to discuss. This will help keep your message short, to the point, and help you write the appropriate subject line.

Use the subject line effectively to get the reader's attention and help them react appropriately. Put the purpose of your e-mail in the form of a phrase (not one word), in the subject line.

People tend to handle first any e-mails that look easy or quick. Make your first paragraph no longer than two or three lines. Keep your message short—a few paragraphs—if possible.

If your e-mail is going to be more than one screen include an attachment. This will make your e-mail look easy, like a fax cover sheet. Your e-mail will then give the reader direction regarding the attachment.

Always include a deadline, in the form of a question, and your reason(s) for the deadline. Mark your e-mail as urgent only if it's really urgent. *Example: Could you please return your time cards by this Friday so you can be paid next week?*

Write e-mail messages as if they were letters or memos. Don't use shortcuts or symbols. Don't type in all caps or all lower case. Use simple formats and avoid fancy backgrounds. Your style and language should be appropriate to your knowledge of the recipient and/or the subject.

Don't write anything that you wouldn't say in person. E-mail is admissible in a court of law, so use the phone if the matter is sensitive.

Create a signature to help recipients: Provide alternative ways for people to contact you. It should include your mailing address and phone number. Keep it to six lines or fewer.

Give instructions with forwards: If you must forward a message, put your comments at the top, either in the subject line or the first paragraph. This saves the recipient time and gets better results. "FYI" doesn't really tell the recipient anything.

Always review each message before you send it: Make sure it's complete, concise, and organized logically. Verify the grammar and spelling. Set up spell check to help catch mistakes—but don't trust it to do the job for you.

"Consider carefully what you write and who may read it eventually. If the president of your company received your e-mail, what would he or she think?"

☑ *Manage incoming calls*

*P*hone calls undermine time management. Many are unnecessary or take longer than necessary. Reduce the calls you take and the time they take from you.

Keep a phone log for a week. Note the time, the caller's name, the purpose of the call, and the duration. Then, evaluate your log. Which calls were absolutely necessary? Could you have delegated any? How can you reduce your time on each call?

Screen your calls, at least during your "veggie time," if it's not necessary for you to answer every call. If you have an assistant, first thing in the morning provide and explain your schedule so he or she knows how to prioritize callers. If you don't have an assistant, use voice mail.

If you answer a call, ask, "What can I do for you?" Encourage the caller to get to the point quickly. Ask questions until you determine the purpose of the call.

Then, decide how the call relates to your priorities. Is it worth interrupting your current task to handle immediately? Can you call the person back at a time that fits your schedule and is appropriate to the priority of the call?

If someone else could handle the call better, either because it's low priority or because you don't have the information, provide the name and number of the person who can help or offer to forward the call to that person. Here are some other hints:

- Save time by using your voice mail more effectively.
- Change your greeting daily or at least weekly, to give your schedule for that day or that week.
- Ask callers to please leave their name, number, reason for the call, and the best time to call back. (Explain that doing so will enable you to call back sooner with the desired help or information.)
- Provide options: another phone number or a pager number for reaching you, the name and number of another person to call, and voice mail.

Three suggestions for managing incoming calls:

Make it easy and efficient: Let people know the best time to reach you and the times to avoid. Also, provide the names and numbers of any coworkers whom they can call instead.

Insist on the essentials: When somebody says, "I'll call you," reply, "OK, and if you don't get me, leave your name and number, remind me why you're calling, and let me know the best time to reach you."

Set aside time to return calls: This is especially smart for lower-priority calls. Generally, it works best to batch them from 11:30 a.m. to noon and at the end of the day.

"On the average, one out of every two business calls is not about business. The telephone is an interruption. You stop your work when it rings ..., so you have to learn how to manage it."

☑ *Master outgoing calls*

*P*rioritize your calls. Then, try to figure out the best time to call—and if you need to talk with a person.

If you're calling to provide or request information and don't need to speak with the other person, try to pick a time when he or she won't be there, so you can just leave a message.

Set aside specific times to make calls, in batches. Make the most important calls in the morning. Batch lower-priority calls from 11:30 a.m. to noon and at the end of the day. People are quicker on the phone before lunch and before they're leaving for the day. Return all voice mail messages within 24 hours, the same day if possible.

Plan every call. That's the smartest way to save time on calls you make. Write down the points to cover and prepare all necessary information. Know how long you expect to take for your points. Keep the call focused.

Anticipate any questions the other person is likely to ask and prepare an answer, along with any information needed. You'll seem more professional and save time.

Check the time before calling and then keep track while you're on the phone. Specifically,

- Start by giving your reason(s) for calling—and then get to your points and stick with them.
- When you've achieved the goal(s) of your call, politely end the call.

- Summarize the call and ask, "Does that cover everything?" Then, my favorite, say, "I know you're really busy, so I'm going to let you go."

If the other person is too busy to talk, make an appointment to call back. Write it down—and make sure that the other person writes it down, too.

Be prepared to leave a message. When you leave a voice mail, keep your message short—15 to 30 seconds. Speak slowly and clearly. Give your name and number, your reason for calling, the best time to call back, and a deadline for reaching you.

Here are three more suggestions for making phone calls:

Make notes on your Master List: When you talk on the phone, keep track, especially of agreements and commitments, for future reference.

Choose voice mail if possible: If someone offers to take a message, ask for voice mail so you can leave a more detailed message and it will get through accurately: "It would probably be easier for you if I could leave a voice mail message."

Return all calls from salespeople: Leave a message that you're not interested or you'll call if interested. This should eliminate future calls from those people—a good investment of a few seconds.

"On average, an unplanned phone call takes five minutes longer than one that has been planned. Planning a phone call can be as easy as a 30-second outline of what you want to say or ask."

—Gary Lockwood

☑ *Delegate*

---

*D*elegation is a very effective means of time management. Unfortunately, many of us don't do it enough.

Why not? We may feel that we can do tasks faster and better than anyone else. We may think that it takes too much time and effort to delegate. We may be afraid that our employees will make mistakes— or even that they'll succeed. We may be control freaks, unwilling to share tasks. We may lack faith in our employees.

But there are compelling benefits, for you and for your employees—beyond the time management benefits. Delegation allows you to focus on the tasks that require your managerial skills. Delegation is a great way to develop employees and motivate them. Delegation shows that you're committed to improving your team: the top skill of great managers is the ability to train employees.

Accept that others can do some jobs as well as you—and maybe better. Then, delegate smart, following these guidelines:

- Before you begin, make a list of all the tasks for which you're currently responsible.
- Decide which tasks or projects will benefit the company or division (tasks that mean something), will improve your abilities or performance, or will benefit a subordinate's knowledge and confidence.
- Don't delegate poorly defined tasks or projects where there's a high risk of failure or that require management involvement or decision.

When delegating, choose the right person for the job. Make sure that he or she has the proper training, experience, and/or knowledge for the job. Tell why you've chosen him or her and why this task is important. Delegate the whole task, if possible—not just what you don't want to do. If that would be too difficult for your employee, start with pieces.

Define the task and specify the results desired and any expectations. Provide guidelines and examples of what's expected, as appropriate.

Set a start time and a deadline. Allow sufficient time. Schedule a midway meeting to discuss progress/issues and don't hover or keep checking with the person every five minutes. Trust.

Make sure that the person understands the tasks or project. Answer any questions. Finally, and most important, give him or her the authority necessary to do the job.

At the conclusion of the job, discuss the results with the person. Praise him or her for the results, discuss any issues, and offer constructive feedback.

To delegate smart, do the following:

Delegate—don't dump: Empower and motivate your employees. Delegation is one of the highest forms of motivation.

Show your confidence: When you delegate, tell your employee that you have confidence in him or her—and then show it by allowing your employee the freedom to take responsibility for the job. Part of the responsibility is to seek you out if any questions or issues arise. Don't micro-manage.

Track the tasks: Use your calendar or your Master List to keep track of the tasks you're delegating.

"There is a great man who makes every man feel small. But the really great man makes every man feel great."
—*Chinese proverb*

☑ *Plan meetings smart*

We're all familiar with the characteristics of unproductive meetings. They're longer. More of them are needed. They're unstructured. Participants arrive unprepared. Participants don't work together. Participants leave frustrated. Follow-up is poor.

We can start improving meetings by planning smart. Ask, is this meeting really necessary? That's the first and most important question. Why meet? There are three basic purposes for meetings: to provide information, to solve problems or make decisions, and to brainstorm.

Calculate the cost of a meeting. Is it possible to serve your purpose in another way? Consider alternatives. For example, if your purpose is to convey information, such as news and reports, maybe e-mail would be better.

Meet only if there's a reason. That may seem obvious, but many meetings are "regular meetings"—every week or even every day, same time, same place, same old.... Regularity is not a reason for meeting.

If you decide that a meeting is necessary, use your purpose(s) to determine whom to invite, how long it should take, and when to schedule it.

Include in the meeting only people who need to be there. Then, tell each participant why you're including him or her. Participants will take greater responsibility in preparing and participating.

Determine the points to cover, how you will handle each, and how long it will take. The length of the meeting should depend on the purpose(s). In general, try to keep it under 90 minutes, which is the average person's attention span.

Here are some additional suggestions for meetings:

Question regular meetings: If you attend any meetings, think about the reasons. Routines can be good or bad. Good regular meetings can be great; ordinary regular meetings can waste time and bore participants.

Know why you're included: When someone includes you in a meeting, find out what's expected of you. Could you send someone else instead or provide information in another way? Could you attend just part of the meeting?

Think "investment": Meetings cost real money. If participants think in terms of dollars per minute, they will likely invest more thought and energy in their meetings, to make them more effective and more efficient, for a better return on investment.

"90% of businesspeople surveyed said half the time they spend in meetings could have been spent more productively. The average employee loses 31 hours a month in unproductive meetings."

☑ *Schedule meetings smart*

Once you've planned your meeting, set a start time and an end time. Do not schedule a meeting for the same day: such meetings tend to be less structured, last longer, and accomplish less. Check the participants' schedules and don't put your meeting immediately before or after any other.

It's generally best to meet in the afternoon. Participants tend to be better prepared, since they can use lunchtime to get ready. They're likely to have gotten at least four hours of work out of the way, so they're less distracted. Above all, don't schedule meetings for the first thing in the day or on Mondays. Friday afternoon may be a good bet; you want to review the progress that week and get everyone on the same page for next week.

I suggest scheduling meetings to start at odd times, such as 2:10 rather than 2:00. For many, "2:00" means "around 2:00," but "2:10" definitely means 2:10.

Create an agenda. State clear objectives; the more specific, the more focused participants will be. Use the "veggie principle" to prioritize the agenda. Schedule times for each point. Distribute the agenda at least a day in advance, so the participants can prepare.

Assign roles to participants. Here are some possibilities:

- leader/facilitator: to conduct the meeting according to the agenda
- note taker: to take notes and then write them up and distribute them within one day after the meeting

- timer: to keep the meeting on schedule
- door person: to close the door when the meeting begins and admit and update any latecomers

Send out a reminder to the participants 30 minutes before the meeting. It's smart to reiterate your reasons for including them, either in your reminder or as they arrive for the meeting. This helps ensure that all participants really participate.

Here are three suggestions for meetings scheduled by others:

Be careful about committing: Don't commit to meetings or conference calls first thing in the morning; make exceptions only for "veggies" and emergencies. In particular, avoid meetings and conference calls Monday mornings. Don't commit to meetings back to back; allow some time between meetings to recuperate and prepare.

Schedule some free time after each meeting: Plan for time so you can use the bathroom, get something to drink or eat, and/or get to your next commitment on time. You're also less likely to stress out if the meeting runs a little long.

Get an agenda: If the person who schedules a meeting doesn't distribute an agenda, ask for one. Expect an agenda for every meeting that includes you—and expect time to prepare for meetings, except in emergencies.

"There is no best time to schedule an unnecessary meeting."
—Anonymous

☑ *Run meetings smart*

You've planned and scheduled the meeting smart. Now, run it smart.

Write the meeting objectives on a white board or a flipchart at the front of the room, so that they focus participants as soon as they arrive.

Start on time. That sets a tone of efficiency. Just close the door and begin the agenda. Let participants know that they can't arrive late. Levy fines, if necessary.

Keep minutes. The person responsible should include the "formal stuff" (such as date, time, leader, purpose, and participants) and then record key points that relate to the agenda. He or she should ask questions to clarify any contributions or decisions.

There should be ground rules: set or review them at the start. They should cover such essentials as showing respect, avoiding distractions, and focusing on the agenda.

Bring up action items from the previous meeting first. Be brief: state the items and sum up the actions taken. Continue the tone of efficiency here.

Keep to the agenda. The number-one reason why meetings don't finish on time is that the leader loses control of the meeting. Schedule non-agenda items for a separate meeting.

Write down the main points or ideas on a flip chart or a white board. Use PowerPoint whenever possible, to generate more interest and ensure greater retention.

End on time or earlier.

After the meeting, remind the note taker to write up and distribute the notes to the participants within one day of the meeting. This is especially important for the action items.

Here are three suggestions for meetings run by others:

Show the respect that you expect: When others are running a meeting, turn off your cell phone and PDA or other devices, avoid any distracting behavior, and don't do any tasks not related to the meeting—even if there are no ground rules.

Participate according to expectations: Know why you were included in the meeting and play your part fully. Make the most of your presence and set a good example.

Leave on time: If someone is running a meeting past the scheduled time, excuse yourself and leave so you can make your next commitment on time. Don't let others control your time. Leaving conveys the message that meetings should be effective and efficient.

"Nobody knows when the first meeting took place, but it's a safe bet that the meeting seemed too long to some participants, poorly organized to others, and boring to at least a few, and it's likely that some were disappointed in the results."

—*Barbara J. Streibel*

About the Author

Kenneth Zeigler is a top expert on time management, organization, and productivity improvement. He has authored many articles on these subjects, and he was the first author to discover the problem is not the system people use but rather their organization skill set.

Ken has served in senior management at firms such as Pillsbury, Hughes, Quaker Oats, Merrill Lynch, and Dean Witter. As a consultant he has advised clients such as Hertz, Hormel, the Federal Reserve, the Comptroller of the Currency, and Fidelity.

Ken attended the University of Minnesota as an undergraduate, where he was a member of the varsity football team, and then completed graduate work in advertising and finance at the University of Illinois. He lives in Nashville with his wife, Mary Beth, and his sons, Zachary and Nicholas.

Visit his Web site at www.kztraining.com.

"Time waste differs from material waste in that there can be no salvage. The easiest of all wastes and the hardest to correct is the waste of time, because wasted time does not litter the floor like wasted material."

—Henry Ford

The McGraw-Hill
Professional Education Series

How to Manage Performance: 24 Lessons for Improving Performance

    By Robert Bacal (0-07-143531-X)

    Goal-focused, commonsense techniques for stimulating greater productivity in the workplace and fostering true commitment.

Dealing with Difficult People: 24 Lessons for Bringing Out the Best in Everyone

    By Rick Brinkman and Rick Kirschner (0-07-141641-2)

    Learn about the 10 types of problem people and how to effectively respond to them to improve communication and collaboration.

How to Motivate Every Employee: 24 Proven Tactics to Spark Productivity in the Workplace

    By Anne Bruce (0-07-141333-2)

    By a master motivator and speaker, this book quickly reviews practical ways you can turn on employees and enhance their performance and your own.

Six Sigma for Managers: 24 Lessons to Understand and Apply Six Sigma Principles in Any Organization

    By Greg Brue (0-07-145548-5)

    Introduces the fundamental concepts of Six Sigma and details practical steps to spearhead a Six Sigma program in the workplace.

How To Be a Great Coach: 24 Lessons for Turning on the Productivity of Every Employee

    By Marshall J. Cook (0-07-143529-8)

    Today's most effective coaching methods to dramatically improve the performance of your employees.

Leadership When the Heat's On: 24 Lessons in High Performance Management

    By Danny Cox and John Hoover (0-07-141406-1)

    Learn hands-on techniques for infusing any company with results-driven leadership at every level, especially during times of organizational turmoil.

Networking for Career Success: 24 Lessons for Getting to Know the Right People

    By Diane Darling (0-07-145603-1)

    Learn the steps for making mutually beneficial career connections and the know-how to cultivate those connections for the benefit of everyone involved.

Why Customers Don't Do What You Want Them To: 24 Solutions to Common Selling Problems

    By Ferdinand Fournies (0-07-141750-8)

    This results-focused guidebook will help you to recognize and resolve twenty common selling problems and objections and help you move beyond them.

The New Manager's Handbook: 24 Lessons for Mastering Your New Role

By Morey Stettner (0-07-141334-0)

Here are 24 quick, sensible, and easy-to-implement practices to help new managers succeed from day one.

Finance for Non-Financial Managers: 24 Lessons to Understand and Evaluate Financial Health

By Katherine Wagner (0-07-145090-4)

This guide offers a bundle of lessons to clearly explain financial issues in layman's terms.

The Handbook for Leaders: 24 Lessons for Extraordinary Leadership

By John H. Zenger and Joseph Folkman (0-07-143532-8)

A workplace-tested prescription for encouraging the behaviors and key drivers of effective leadership, from one of today's top training teams.

Outside the U.S., order multiple copies of McGraw-Hill Professional Education titles from:

Asia
McGraw-Hill Education (Asia)
Customer Service Department
60 Tuas Basin Link
Singapore 638775
Tel: (65) 6863 1580
Fax: (65) 6862 3354
E-mail: mghasia@mcgraw-hill.com

Australia and New Zealand
McGraw-Hill Australia Pty Ltd
82 Waterloo Road
North Ryde, NSW 2113, Australia
Tel: +61-2-9900-1800
Fax: +61-2-9878-8881
E-mail: CService_Sydney@mcgraw-hill.com

Canada
Special Sales Representative, Trade Division
McGraw-Hill Ryerson Limited
300 Water Street
Whitby, Ontario L1N 9B6
Canada
Tel: 1-800-565-5758

Europe, Middle East, Africa
McGraw-Hill Professional, EMEA
Shoppenhangers Road, Maidenhead
Berkshire SL6 2QL
United Kingdom
Tel: +44 (0)1628 502 975
Fax: +44 (0)1628 502 167
E-mail: emma_gibson@mcgraw-hill.com

Other Areas
For other markets outside the U.S., please e-mail Bonnie Chan at
bonnie_chan@mcgraw-hill.com.

Getting Organized at Work
Order Form

1–99 copies	_____ copies @ $7.95 per book
100–499 copies	_____ copies @ $7.75 per book
500–999 copies	_____ copies @ $7.50 per book
1,000–2,499 copies	_____ copies @ $7.25 per book
2,500–4,999 copies	_____ copies @ $7.00 per book
5,000–9,999 copies	_____ copies @ $6.50 per book
10,000 or more copies	_____ copies @ $6.00 per book

Name _____

Title _____

Organization _____

Phone (____)_____

Street address _____

City/State (Country) _____ Zip _____

Fax (____)_____

Purchase order number (if applicable) _____

Applicable sales tax, shipping, and handling will be added.

☐ VISA ☐ MasterCard ☐ American Express

Account number _____ Exp. date ____

Signature _____

Or call 1-800-842-3075
Corporate, Industry, & Government Sales

The McGraw-Hill Companies, Inc.
2 Penn Plaza
New York, NY 10121